Making a Castle

You will need:

- one big box

- four cans, all the same size

- colored paper to put on the box
  and around the cans

- colored paper, cut into strips

- a circle of colored paper,

  to make into four cones

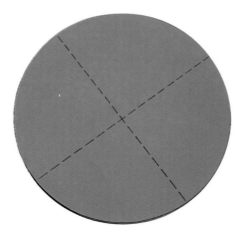

The Castle Walls

Put colored paper

on the outside of the box.

Cut four strips of paper, like this:

Tape them onto the top of the box.

The Towers

Cut some colored paper

into four rectanales.

Put the paper around the cans.

Step 1:

Step 2:

Step 3:

Cut four strips of paper, like this:

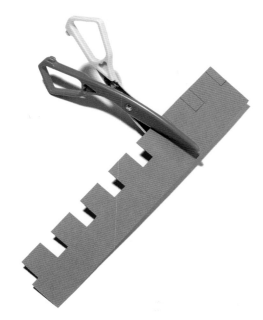

Tape them around the tops

of the four cans.

The Cones

Cut the circle into quarters.

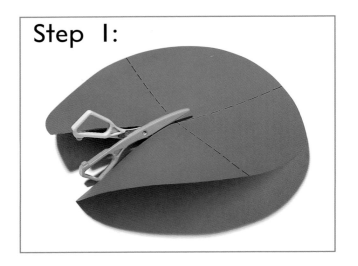

Step 1:

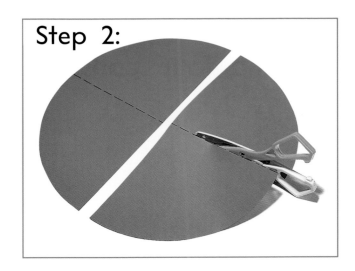

Step 2:

Make the quarters into cones.

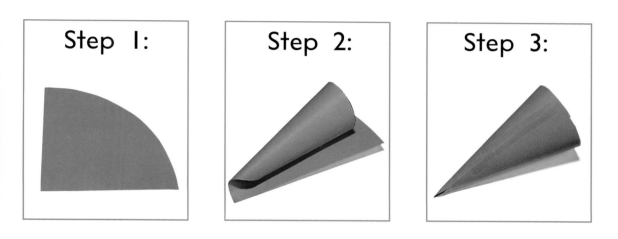

Step 1:

Step 2:

Step 3:

The four cones will look like this:

The Castle

All the parts have been made,
you just have to put them together!

Draw a rectangle on the box.
Make it look like a door.

Draw small rectangles on the box.
Make them look like windows.

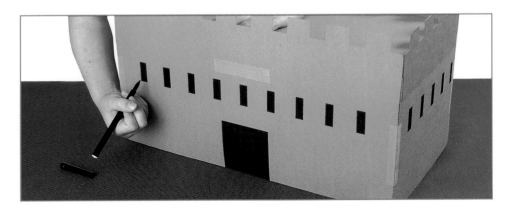

Draw some smaller rectangles
on the towers.

Make them look like windows, too.

Put the four cans on top of the box.

They go in the four corners.

Put the cones on the cans.

Now you have made a castle!

Make a box, a can, and a cone

A box
You need:
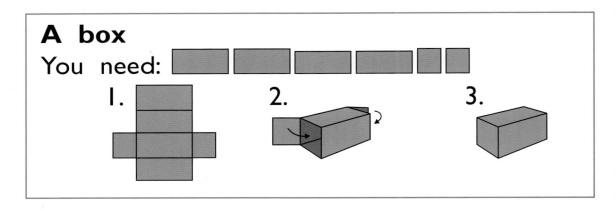

1.
2.
3.

A can
You need:
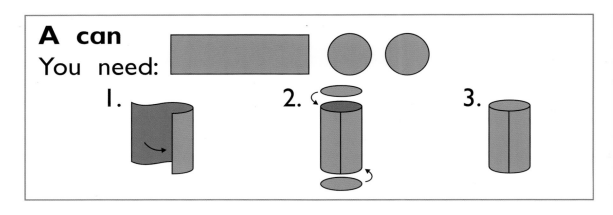

1.
2.
3.

A cone
You need:
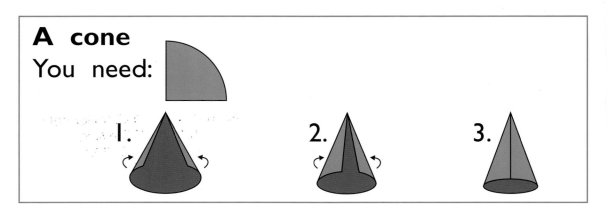

1.
2.
3.